☆ ☆ ☆

INTRODUCTION

TO

LIP READING

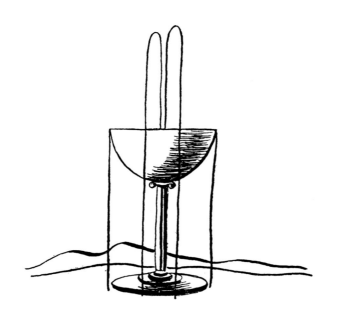

BETTER LIVING FOUNDATION
NEW YORK

Copyright 1939
Better Living Foundation, Inc.
20 West 45th Street
New York, N. Y.
All rights reserved

Printed in U.S.A.

CONTENTS

CHAPTER	PAGE
FOREWORD	5
I LIP READING AS A KEY TO LIFE	7
II THE CHALLENGE OF IMPAIRED HEARING	13
III THE PAST AND PRESENT OF LIP READING	20
IV LIP READING AND SELF-DEVELOPMENT	23
V INSTRUCTIONS FOR THE NEW STUDENT	33
VI LESSONS FOR HOME PRACTICE	40

FOREWORD

This book is one of a series prepared as practical guide books for the individual who is faced with the problems raised by inefficient hearing.

All volumes in the Better Living Series have been written by recognized authorities in a particular field, or the material has been gathered from a number of authoritative sources by trained researchers and then carefully edited to arrive at a form which may be readily mastered and applied by any intelligent reader.

Other titles in the Better Living Series are: *Your Hearing and Your Health, Educating Your Hearing, How to Improve Your Speech, Success and Security* (dealing with vocational problems) and *A Personal Inventory* (a guide to self-knowledge and adjustment).

Throughout the preparation of these volumes, the editors have been guided by the hope that in the faithful execution of the extensive task of bringing together information from so many sources, and arranging it in usable form, they will be making a definite contribution to one of the great needs of our time — namely to close the gap between available knowledge and its actual application by the average man for his benefit. This need is nowhere more greatly evident than in respect to hearing impairment.

May the reader find in the following pages, therefore, a key which will unlock for him at least one of the doors to a happier and more abundant life. It should be his constant inspiration to know that there are relatively few indeed who cannot today surmount the handicaps of impaired hearing. The knowledge and the means are at hand; the rest is up to him, a challenge to his will and determination to persevere and overcome, encouraged by the knowledge that what thousands of others have done, he too can achieve.

BETTER LIVING FOUNDATION

New York, N. Y.

CHAPTER I

LIP READING AS A KEY TO LIFE

WE human beings are essentially gregarious creatures and the give-and-take of our daily contacts serves in large measure to keep us normal. To be able to understand when some neighbor makes a trite remark about the weather, or asks some time-worn question about our health is of more vital importance to our happiness and self-esteem than can possibly be realized until that ability has taken wing. It is cold comfort to be told that most of the talk of the world is mere chatter, gossip, twaddle. We should prefer to make our own estimates of the conversations that go on about us. We want to take part. We want to be in the ring and not standing on the side lines trying to catch an idea, be it spicy gossip or profound philosophy.

Some years ago a delightful book was published by the wife of Viscount Grey. She tells of a boy, her own little son, who was highly imaginative and exceedingly clever about getting his own way. He liked to lie in bed in the morning and resented his nurse's attempts to get him up. One morning when she came to his bedside, he exclaimed, "You mustn't touch me."

"Why?" she asked.

"Because I am a flower and mustn't be picked," he replied.

Coming into his room the following morning, the nurse greeted him with, "Well, are you a flower again that mustn't be picked?"

"No," was the answer. "I am a stamp that's stuck down."

8 INTRODUCTION TO LIP READING

Now nobody wants to be a stamp stuck down to deafness, but if we are to be liberated it is we ourselves who must take action. We must set about our own rehabilitation. We must achieve the extrovert point of view. We must learn how to find our places in the general scheme of society. Deafness, total or partial, necessitates reorientation. "To a frog in a well," says an old Chinese proverb, "heaven is only a sieve in size." If we prefer, our heaven can be quite as small as the frog's.

It is noticeable that in any large audience everyone adjusts himself so as to be able to see the speaker. The man behind the post changes his place; the lady behind the large hat asks that the obstruction to seeing be removed. It is not only hearing but also seeing that the great majority of people desire. Certainly this fact is not based on mere curiosity as to the appearance of the speaker, the length of the nose, the color of the tie, whether or not the costume is in the latest fashion. The point is that more immediate comprehension and truer enjoyment result from the use of both hearing and seeing. This is the natural combination, the ear and the eye communicating simultaneously with the brain. Where there is impairment of the hearing apparatus, the eye supplements the ear with quite amazing success. How logical it is then that those using hearing aids in conjunction with an expert use of lip reading should be the ones who most completely triumph over deafness. It is not simply that they more readily understand the spoken word but that they somehow seem more natural; they use their instruments with such ease and grace that to all intents and purposes they are hearing people and those who hear normally forget that they are deafened. Perhaps the most gratifying compliment that can be given to us underhearing folks is this, "I never think of you as being deaf."

When suggesting a course of lip reading to a hard of hearing acquaintance, one is often met by the reply, "Oh, I am not deaf enough for that. I get along pretty well. I'll wait until I can't hear." As a matter of fact, the study of lip reading should be undertaken in the very early stages of deafness; first because helpful habits should at once be established and again because it is well known that many cases of deafness are progressive and the need of lip reading may become more and more imperative. This resistance psychology of the hard of hearing is almost universal and it is not always easy to explain. In the beginning our inclination is to stand stubbornly against the acknowledgment of our handicap; we blame other people for not speaking clearly, for having muffled voices. Next we refuse the most obvious sort of help. Clinging tenaciously to something that is gradually slipping away, we are content to stumble along unaided. We are strangely obdurate, like people who choose the familiar beef stew and prunes and refuse even to taste delicious new foods because they are unfamiliar.

Someone, it is said, once asked Professor Michelson, the great physicist and Nobel prize winner, why he worked so hard over measuring the speed of light and he replied, "Because it is such great fun." Hard work but fun. So it may be with lip reading. It would be unfair to the prospective student to proclaim that lip reading is easily acquired or to pretend that it is a perfect substitute for hearing. Nothing can absolutely replace what has been lost. There is a minority of people to whom lip reading is extremely easy; they are natural lip readers. Yet practically everyone upon noticing a loss in acuity begins to do some lip reading. How often the slightly hard of hearing think that they hear when really they are seeing. With most people, perhaps, the study requires time and effort, but it is surpassingly rewarding. And after all, should a matter of ease or difficulty deter one? Does a youth taking up a course in mathematics, for instance, do so because it is easy or be-

10   INTRODUCTION TO LIP READING

cause it is difficult? He takes the course because he wants to know something about mathematics, he needs that knowledge in his future profession, in his life.

Unquestionably everyone with a hearing loss needs to know something about lip reading and the earlier that knowledge is acquired the smoother will be the road. A man with even a slight impairment of sight equips himself at once with glasses. A man who has sustained a foot injury buys himself a cane or a crutch the better to take his place in the march of time. Yet neither glasses, cane nor crutches are perfect. They help at times almost unbelievably but all of us prefer the equipment that Nature gave us. The mere knowledge, however, that we are not to be left in the lurch in spite of a recognized handicap, can create a kind of renewal of spirit, a personal renaissance which brings a fresh outlook upon the problems that assail us. It is often lip reading, in the case of the hard of hearing, that brings this new spirit; in the course of time it may truly become the "great fun" that Dr. Michelson knew in his labors for science.

Long years ago, lip reading was defined as a subtle art, and as an art it must be approached. He who dreams that it can be memorized like scientific formulae is doomed to disappointment. Like music or painting or sculpture, it imposes the devotion of a lifetime. Neglected, it slips away. Used and enjoyed, it becomes the friend for whom we entertain a deep and grateful affection. Truly it has gifts of many kinds to shower upon its devotees. It can be the cause of our developing a taste for good books. It can open our eyes to the joys of Nature and the world of art. It can bring understanding friends. It can teach us to concentrate upon one field of endeavor where we may win conspicuous success.

On the other hand lip reading makes claims upon us. How casually we used to accept the beauty and wonder of a concert by

Paderewski! How little thought we gave to the years of study and practice that lay behind his magnificent performances! In his recently published Memoirs, he writes of "the incredible hours of practice and concentration" and of "the never-ending finger practice" necessary to the presentation of a single concert. His account of practicing in the old Steinway warehouse on Fourteenth Street in New York City would be amusing were it not so tragic. In a cold, gloomy loft lighted by two candles, he practiced for five hours one November night in 1891 while his secretary and the night watchman snored loudly in the corner. No student of lip reading need ever fear such grueling experiences, but he must understand that being an adequate lip reader presupposes the willingness to work hard and long.

Not only must the student be prepared to give time and effort to the study, but he must also be ready to face the limitations inherent in the art; these the most skilful lip reader would be the first to acknowledge. Reconciled to the fact that his lost hearing cannot be perfectly replaced, he will learn with persistent study that lip reading is an indispensable crutch. There will be times, having mastered the art, when he will read a speaker's lips as easily as a printed page. There will be other less happy times when lip reading will be the mountain climber's Everest.

The ease of his work unfortunately depends upon so many things over which he has no control; the manner in which the speaker uses the organs of speech that reveal most to the lip reader, for example; whether or not the facial expression gives any indication of the thought, for if the face is "expressive of inexpression", to borrow Coleridge's description of his own countenance, the lip reader will have to make almost superhuman efforts. A poor light on the speaker's face may make all the difference between failure and success. Not everyone can read lips at a distance. Most lip readers are distracted by conspicuous gesticulation. To follow a man who paces up and down a platform wagging his head is one of the impossibilities. Yet given advantageous conditions, the lip reader can perform miracles, as only those who cannot hear will unanimously attest.

Any organization for the hard of hearing in the country could cite innumerable instances of people whose lives have been transfigured by the study of lip reading and the experience of the positive, constructive atmosphere of a lip reading class-room. It is no exaggeration to state that women on the verge of nervous breakdowns have discovered in lip reading the anchor that has enabled them to carry on their lives, to serve their families and to become normally happy beings. There are to-day social workers and teachers in the field of serving the hard of hearing who as young girls sat upstairs reading novels while the family entertained guests in the parlor. Conscious of growing deafness, they sought solitude, avoided social contacts and rationalized themselves into the belief that they had very literary tastes. Lip reading was the magic word that opened the door to fuller and more useful lives.

There are men in the business and professional fields who through the influence of some teacher of lip reading have adopted intelligent attitudes toward deafness and courageously taken their places in the company of those who strive for the eradication of the pressing problems of deafness. There are young boys and girls who through lip reading have been enabled to pursue college courses and to fit themselves for careers of service and happiness. Thousands would joyfully bear witness to the practical uses of lip reading as well as to the spiritual uplift that comes with it — the new poise, the self-assurance, the steadiness, the outward and upward look.

CHAPTER II

THE CHALLENGE OF IMPAIRED HEARING

All the world knows that John Keats left an imperishable legacy of poetry. There is one oft-quoted line of his that gives us people with impaired hearing pause. "Heard melodies are sweet but those unheard are sweeter." Beautiful and comforting, yes, but no deaf person would call unheard melodies "sweet." To us they mean pain — pain because we cannot hear. Stalking into our days like a menacing ghost, deafness has brought heartache and embarrassment. It makes us doubt ourselves and our dearest friends. It may, we know, necessitate a complete about-face in our social and economic lives. In the early days when the shadow fell across our paths we knew the blackness of despair.

Time is a miraculous healer and human nature is made of resilient stuff. The fighting spirit inevitably asserts itself as we gradually come to the realization that even if the walls of our house seem to be made of cold, hard facts, there remain the doors and windows that lead out to the world beyond and look up to the firmament above. An inner voice tells us that the surest way to add to the burden of deafness is to assume an attitude of self-pity, to allow ourselves to become suspicious and morbid and, withdrawing from normal contacts, to climb up into an ivory tower of self-centered seclusion. It tells us with equal force that the surest way to lighten the burden is to accept the challenge of deafness wholeheartedly. This means, first of all, that we stand ready to say to the

INTRODUCTION TO LIP READING

world, "I am hard of hearing," and to say it smilingly; then that we take up the good fight, for it IS good to fight and it is stupid not to fight.

In that great book, "Man the Unknown," the need of struggle is constantly emphasized. Privation and hardship, we learn, inure the body to fatigue and sorrow; the will is strengthened in use; mentally and physically man is intended to struggle in order that his character may be developed. Accepting this theory, we under-hearing people might contend that we have a definite advantage over the hearing world. We carry about with us every hour of the day something to make us fight — unless, of course, we are the sort of supine people who lie down under adversity and let it roll over our happiness like a tidal wave of destruction.

Each good soldier in his own sphere of action, under his special conditions of life must make his particular struggle. In our modern world there are two paramount weapons with which every hard of hearing person should take his place in the great army of the un-defeated. One is lip reading and the other is a well-adjusted hearing device. Both are obtainable, in theory at least and generally in practice, by everyone. Both are useful, nay indispensable. The truly intelligent man or woman whose hearing has become impaired will promptly acquire them, knowing that he has taken the wisest precautions against becoming a dull-witted, unsociable human being, assured that by these means he may be delivered from his petty, timid self and attain his rightful heritage of becoming an integrated personality.

One of the great exemplars in the large company of the hard of hearing was Dr. Horace Howard Furness, the eminent Shake-speare scholar. He was a friend of Ralph Waldo Emerson, and does not that fact alone prove that he was no ordinary man? Emerson once said of him that he had "a face like a benediction" and "speech like a benefaction." Great gentleman, scholar and soldier of the spirit, he accepted life with a gallantry and serenity of temper that identify him as one of the noble souls who have walked in the fields where silence reigns. Deafness never separated him from his fellows and to the end of his days he held in a very special degree the love and admiration of all who knew him. His flashing wit, his ready smile, his romantic temperament commanded friendship. In his numerous letters he makes few references to his deafness but one remark concerning it is significant. "I've become as deaf as twenty-seven adders," he writes, "and live a most secluded, humdrum, prosaic and happy life." This was written before the death of his wife when in his family and his work he had found complete happiness in spite of a crushing handicap.

Few of us average mortals are richly endowed like Dr. Furness but there is a way to happiness for us all. In the last analysis the motive for studying lip reading is really happiness. Victory over physical disability, success in holding one's place in society, the sense of independence, the consciousness of making life a little easier and pleasanter for those we hold dear, in all of these lip reading plays a vital part. There can be no shadow of a doubt that more happy people would make a better world nor is there any doubt that thousands of hard of hearing people would be made happier by the study of lip reading. It is a regrettable fact and one against which the medical profession is making a valiant fight that something like one twentieth of the population of our country are sufficiently handicapped by a hearing loss to make communication unreliable. Spiritually and economically what an asset it would be to our national well-being to put more happiness and usefulness into these lives. It sounds like a dream, but might well be reality.

There is assuredly an art of being deaf. What labor and effort lie back of the art need not be published to the world. The main matter is to attain; since deafness is our destiny, we must strive to be as delightfully deafened as lies within human possibilities. Such a statement may seem strange to those who are taking the first steps along the "Road of Silence." These novices must learn that there are hosts of people similarly handicapped who are carrying on with banners flying, who are beloved and admired and without whom life would be a little duller, a little less worth living for their friends.

We are made, of course, by heredity and environment but also by our very own selves. It is we who make our histories, we who make the choices. We are born with a capacity for thought, for judgment. This capacity may be endangered, however, if we allow a crust of unfortunate habits to envelop our beings. The crust of pretense, for instance, may become very thick — pretending to understand, pretending indeed to be something that we are not. Such pretense can be the barrier to our ever fully becoming what we might be. The timid, self-conscious man, anxious about the impression that he is making, nervous lest he be guilty of some unfortunate blunder, how can he hope to express his real self? How can he hope to be his real self? And is there anything more important than being one's real self? The flame of life, which is love and wonder and will and worship, burns in us all — the deafened, the hearing. By the grace of God we are so made that we can rise and relight the flame when it flickers low. An intelligent estimate of our deafness, its effect upon ourselves and those with whom we live will help to light the flame.

Thinking our problems through and acting upon the thought, that is the sane approach. We may not know what thought is but most of us believe that it is the colossal power that moves our days; full well do we know that one avenue of thought is cut off if we are deafened. The world that comes to him who hears is not identical

THE CHALLENGE OF IMPAIRED HEARING 17

with the world that comes to him who hears not. To make these worlds more nearly the same science offers us hearing instruments; education offers us opportunities to train our eyes and our minds to a point where the loss of hearing is infinitely minimized. It is of vital importance that we keep such residual hearing as we possess and that we make use of it; for one reason, it is our best means of keeping our natural voice quality. When tests prove that our hearing is below normal, we should at once set about making use of the best available supplement to a hearing loss and that is lip reading.

Doubtless many people who are hard of hearing in some degree feel as if they were merely existing and perhaps to their normally hearing friends they do appear to be only partly alive. Several years ago Dr. Bowie of Grace Church, New York City, published a book called "On Being Alive." In it he tells of a letter written by a little boy which said, "I send you my love. I hope you will live all your life." The child, of course, meant to say, "live a long life" but what he did say contains the germ of a great truth. Really to *live* all of one's life, could there be a happier wish? If that were really possible for everyone, what a different world this would be! Perhaps it is more possible than we know, even for the hard of hearing who more than most people feel that they cannot live fully and deeply.

Not only the deafened would do well to follow Dr. Bowie's advice — to open our eyes a little wider and look long and attentively at the beauty of Nature; to acknowledge our limitations and ignorances and try to be teachable; to make some positive effort to cultivate our imaginations so that we may be ready for fresh adventures in wonder. His point is well emphasized in his reminder about meteorites — that when one passes a planet with no atmosphere, "it remains a solid chunk," but if it passes a planet with an atmosphere, it bursts into "a shower of stars." There is the choice for every individual — solid chunks or showers of stars.

Some, to be sure, seem to be born lucky. Being born with the gift of appreciation, for instance, would go far in making the world starry for us. In his "Autobiography with Letters," Professor William Lyon Phelps states that it is his capacity for enjoyment that has made his life what it is — and few more abundant, more useful lives could be named. Someone, indeed, has dubbed him "The Great American Appreciator." He says in one place that "the way to appreciate beauty is to keep looking at it; to appreciate music is to keep listening to it; to appreciate poetry is to keep reading it." This would seem to indicate that even with the gift of appreciation bestowed by the gods, there still remains the necessity of effort. This is the kind of effort that lip readers must ceaselessly make. Lip reading demands the constant doing of the thing, the unrelenting keeping-at-it. The priceless things of life are not handed to us on silver platters. They are won with spurs on. The will must be called into use. A motto on an old sun dial reads, "Make the passing shadow serve thy will."

Yet almost instinctively every hard of hearing person does make for himself a kind of armor with which to meet the world. In the early stages of deafness we learn little ways of protecting ourselves, of avoiding embarrassing situations. We are uncertain of the exact price that has been quoted. A dollar and — ? We hand out two dollars; that is sure. And this is not by any means to suggest that we of imperfectly functioning ears invariably have an ample supply of dollars! It does rightly suggest however, that we have faith in the honesty of the average man. Besides he does not know what *we* do not know! In asking questions, we early learn the value of the direct form. "Can I get to the post office by the subway?" The answer in most cases will be "Yes" or "No." In choosing a seat in a room where we are to engage in conversation, we choose the chair where the light will be on the other people's faces—providing, of course, that we can do so without discommoding anyone. At home, in the office, we sit with our backs to the light. We train our families to get our attention before addressing us at length. Indeed there are countless little tricks that contribute to our ease in meeting the world, little tricks that no hearing man would even dream of and that would utterly amaze him if he knew but the half of the other man's case. Ah, yes, we hard of hearing folk have our little ways, our mild subterfuges and we can be really clever and very quick-witted but we don't talk about it very much. We are contented just to get by.

CHAPTER III

THE PAST AND PRESENT OF LIP READING

All of the artifices in the world, however, and the greatest of cleverness will not serve the purpose of lip reading. It is not a little strange that lip reading has only recently taken its rightful place in the education of the hard of hearing. The totally deaf have had consideration and educational opportunities for centuries, but the hard of hearing, for the most part, have been consistently neglected, pushed to the wall, shoved into corners and relegated to Deck E on the ship of life.

Actually lip reading was known in several of the countries of Europe before 1500 but it was not taught, in all probability, until the latter years of the 16th century. Up to that time those who could read the lips were thought to be miraculously endowed.

It was a Spanish Benedictine monk who first made a success of teaching the deaf. Pedro Ponce de Leon died in 1584. The registry of his monastery contains this statement: "Slept in the Lord, Brother Pedro Ponce, benefactor of this house, who amongst other virtues, which he possessed in high degree, excelled chiefly in this, which is held in the greatest estimation by the whole world, to wit, teaching the dumb to speak."

In the 17th century the recognition of the deaf man's intelligence came almost simultaneously in Holland, Belgium and England as well as Spain, and his education was undertaken. As the old records phrase it, he was taught "to listen with the eye." In England the first great authority was John Bulwer, a physician who published a book about deafness in 1648. It was he who called lip reading the "subtile art" and he made extravagant claims for it, but undoubtedly he knew a great deal about the problems of the deafened. He states that articulate speech "does not necessarily require the audible sound of the voyce." He declared that there is an "ear situated in the eie."

The 18th century brought the Abbé de l'Epée who gave a lifetime of devoted effort to the deaf and whose monument stands today in front of the Institution for the Deaf in Paris. It brought also Samuel Heinicke, who used an oral method and who believed in teaching the deaf to speak because "clear thought is possible only by speech." No matter of interest escaped the great mind of Samuel Johnson. He writes of visiting a famous school for the deaf in Edinburgh conducted by Thomas Braidwood and he remarks that the pupils "know so well what is spoken that it is an expression scarcely figurative to say they hear with the eye."

In the United States the first publication about deafness was in 1793. The author, William Thornton, was an advocate of lip reading, insisting that the art was "very obtainable." Yet with the European background of education for the deafened and a number of more or less sporadic efforts to establish schools and classes here in America, it seems almost incredible that in 1860 there was "no teacher of articulation" in all the broad land. The first school was opened in Northampton, Massachusetts, in 1867. It was the outgrowth of work done with three little deaf girls and it constituted a triumph for the oral method.

One of the best friends and the greatest benefactors of the deafened in America was Alexander Graham Bell, the eminent scientist, who in endeavoring to invent something to make his wife hear, discovered the principles of the telephone. In 1899 Dr. Bell founded the Volta Review, an illustrated magazine for educators and parents of the deaf and for the hard of hearing. In 1913 only three schools of lip reading were advertised in this periodical. In 1917 there were 48 in 26 different states, and by 1931 public school classes had been organized in 96 of the larger cities.

The American Society for the Hard of Hearing was founded in 1919. This Society remains to-day the only national society dedicated to the service of the hard of hearing. One of its major aims is the spread of the gospel of lip reading among both children and adults. The growing movement in behalf of the deafened has received its impetus chiefly from the deafened themselves. This is perhaps a unique instance of a group of handicapped people forming an organization for the amelioration of the handicap from which they themselves suffer. At last this large and important class of people are emerging from their preoccupation with their limitations and tragedies and are banded together for loyal and enthusiastic service in a cause for which they have special sympathy and understanding.

There are, nevertheless, too many people of intelligence to whom lip reading means very little. Well-informed physicians, educators and social workers know its value and its uses but many of the well-educated have no definite ideas as to how the subject is taught or what results may reasonably be expected from it. They may be familiar with Poor Richard's advice, "When you speak to a man, look in his eyes. When he speaks to you, look in his mouth." The chances are that they have never given this idea of looking in the mouth a second thought. Benjamin Franklin was one of the wisest men who ever lived but probably even he did not fully realize how excellent was his admonition.

Chapter IV

LIP READING AND SELF-DEVELOPMENT

Results in lip reading, it goes without saying, vary greatly, depending upon the student's type of mind and in general upon his character. Yet every earnest teacher holds a very definite aim; she knows what she would like to give her students by way of equipment for his contacts with his fellows. Just what his reaction will be she cannot tell at the outset; while she does not expect miracles, she knows what magnificently constructive help has come to many who have entered into training in the subtle art. Thus her wishes for her student would run something like this; she would give him well-developed powers of concentration and of observation; quickness and accuracy in the use of his eyes; ready intuitions and synthetic powers that enable him to combine elements into a whole; familiarity with hundreds of visible words and the ability to recognize them on the lips; an enlarged vocabulary; broader interests; a pleasant, intelligent facial expression; and a sense of humor. It is a far-reaching program and depends for success much more upon the student than upon the instructor. Yet only the very clever, natural lip readers succeed without the help of a trained teacher. She it is who lays the broad foundations on which the student will build his accomplishments. She sets his feet on the right path and points the way that he must go.

The power of concentration is something in which many people are almost entirely deficient. Teachers more than most people know how many scatter-brains there are in the world. For the would-be lip reader concentration is the first essential; without it he cannot learn to read the lips. He must have it or acquire it in a form as well-developed as, let us say, the Scotchman who went up in an airplane with his wife. The understanding was that he would not have to pay the fares if neither of them spoke. So successful was the gentleman, as the story runs, in concentrating on silence, that he did not speak even when his wife fell out of the plane.

In general those with a hearing impairment soon learn to make extra use of their eyes. As a man who loses his right hand quickly learns to use his left hand in new ways, as the blind make special use of their ears, so the hard of hearing instinctively begin to hear with their eyes. Even a slight facility in eye work is a very positive help, while well-rounded training of the eyes brings invaluable assistance. Not all deafened people by any means enjoy the theatre, but those who care for it derive a great deal of their pleasure from sight alone. The visual memory of many of the deafened is unusually strong so that they can describe with considerable accuracy a scene that has made only a vague, general impression on those who have distinctly heard the spoken lines. Ideally, at least, the hard of hearing man's ardor for the beauty of Nature and the world of art should be especially deep and satisfying. In this direction lies the compensation for that portion of the aesthetic world that has passed away with the loss of hearing.

One of the tragedies of deafness is that it brings indifference. We cease to make an effort and sink down into a slough of unconcern. Willingly we become dull plodders, lacking any spark of enthusiasm, any keen interests, any deep desires. Nothing touches us very potently, nothing matters. It is easier not to care, we say to ourselves. Obviously this is the way of least resistance, the effortless way; obviously it reacts very unfortunately, yea disastrously upon our personalities. What we need is someone with a big stick to stir us up, to train our minds, to force us to make use of our eyes, to inspire us with the will to act and not to be downed. In almost everyone the eye can be trained for greater speed and accuracy. The reaches of the human mind are well nigh infinite. The personality that is acutely aware, that is deeply responsive, that has mind and eye disciplined to the limit of use will travel a long way on the "Road of Silence."

Women, as a rule, have more highly developed intuitions than men. Some women are positively uncanny, as every husband knows. They seem to understand what you are going to say before you have half completed your sentence. This keen intuition is undoubtedly one of a woman's advantages over man in the field of lip reading. Statistics would doubtless show that there are more women who study lip reading than men. There are certainly very few if any men in the ranks of the national champions of lip reading. This is not to say that men cannot become more intuitive if they make the effort to educate this highly desirable faculty.

Again he who comes to lip reading with a *synthetic* mind is the happy possessor of an invaluable mental power. He who comes with an *analytical* mind, on the other hand, will surely meet obstacles. He will probably become impatient and discouraged if he is uncertain about the minor words that only serve to string the important words together. He must be trained to grasp the whole thought, using his imagination and his knowledge of sentence structure. As a pianist reads the composer's phrase and not each note, so the lip reader must learn not to pause for one word but to aim at the general idea. From the start the teacher will see to it that analytical habits are broken down and synthetic habits built up.

Those with normal hearing think little or nothing about the visibility or invisibility of words. They do not need to, to be sure. To

26 INTRODUCTION TO LIP READING

the lip reader this is a crucial matter, as crucial as to the aviator the matter of being able to see his way across the sky. A succession of invisible words may leave a lip reader in a perfect cloud-bank of confusion; while visible words may carry him on soaring wings to the desired goal of easy comprehension. Many sounds in our language are so formed as to be readily seen and every hard of hearing person should know them as surely as he knows that two and two make four. Not only that, he should know what he cannot be expected to see so that he will become expert in making mental substitutions for the blank passages that strike the eye in practically every spoken sentence.

Knowledge of this negative side of lip reading is of more importance than one would guess. For example the movements of the lips for "f" and "v" and "sh" and that of the tongue for "th" are like traffic lights for a good lip reader. He never misses such words as "father", "fish", "shadow", "show" and scores of others. The recognition of such words being very easy for him, he can reserve his greater mental effort for things not so easy.

Could there be anything more intelligent for a hard of hearing individual to do than to learn to recognize these visible movements? Golfers young and old use every means to learn the newest rules of their game. And who is more avid of knowing the latest rules than the gray-haired bridge player? Certainly age does not hinder their going back to school to learn something. But somehow we hard of hearing folk hesitate about learning the newest rules in the game of deafness. While trained teachers all over the country stand ready to teach us, we make every kind of excuse to procrastinate. Yes, that ancient and inveterate thief of time stands at our elbow, and the best thing for us to do is serenely to turn our backs upon him and march off to be taught.

It goes without saying that the lip reader will be slow to see words that are unfamiliar to him. If he has never heard of Fujiyama the chances are that he will not see the word on the lips. If he does not know that General Gamelin is head of the French army, he will probably not understand that somewhat difficult name when spoken. If he does not read the newspapers and magazines and keep in touch with the vocabulary of everyday writing and speaking, (current slang included), he will find difficulty in understanding much of the conversation that goes on about him. His wisest procedure is to acquire a large working vocabulary, ideally a little larger than that in general use among those with whom he associates. He should keep one jump ahead, perhaps two. He should indeed be ready at all times to introduce topics of conversation and he should have the language with which to express his ideas clearly. In all schools of lip reading the student learns these things. He is stimulated to read widely. He is drilled on vocabularies of common usage. Continually he is urged and helped to gain a command of language.

The question of good and bad habits is a large one, and each student presents an individual problem to the teacher. The object is always to break down the habits that militate against successful lip reading and to replace them with habits that will contribute to ease of understanding. For instance the habit of interrupting at missed words can be supplanted by the very helpful habit of waiting until the end of a sentence (or it may be a long clause) when the thought has been completed and when every chance of seeing key words has been exhausted.

Always the student must remember that what he wants is ideas, not just separate words. If you stop to think of it, hearing people are doing exactly the same thing; their conversation is an exchange of ideas and the words that convey them are secondary. Another faulty habit of the hard of hearing is that of monopolizing the conversation. Because the lip reader has his trained eyes and mind to depend upon, he is more ready to listen, less avid of doing all the talking himself. Certainly, greeting people with long monologues is only adding more bricks to the wall of deafness. No matter how brilliantly we can discourse, we must learn to give the other fellow his chance in the universal game of talk.

Perhaps the acquisition of a larger vocabulary would indicate wider interests; but the wider interests are to be encouraged for yet another reason, namely in order to fill the mind with worth-while ideas and to lead the thoughts outward into the marvelous world where we live. In so doing, we minimize the trials caused by deafness and set about making ourselves of some use in our particular place in the sun.

Go to any established school of lip reading and you will find that after the first stages in the study of lip reading have been passed, the material offered is of an informative and cultural nature. Many sentence drills relate to history, current events, books, scientific discovery; they have to do with what is of perennial interest and inspiration. Advanced students attend lectures and informal talks. One day it will be a discussion of the drama with a resumé of a new play, perhaps. Another day it may be a review of a best seller or a talk on the life of some famous musician or some great artist. A woman coming out of one such lecture class where she had followed the thought entirely by lip reading was heard to exclaim, "It gives me such a sense of power!" If deafness had ever caused an inferiority complex in that woman, she had well recovered. Another woman who had been attending a school of lip reading for several years remarked to a friend, "Why, I am getting a college education." Exaggeration, yes, but could anyone doubt what that school was doing for that woman's mind and spirit?

In the Chronicles of the Venerable Bede (who died as you may remember in 735) there is an account of a "dumme" youth to whom

LIP READING AND SELF-DEVELOPMENT 29

speech was restored and as a result his "countinance" became "amyable and pleausaunt to behold". Teachers of lip reading everywhere behold this miracle of the changed countenance. Almost without exception people growing deaf show the strain in a troubled, tense facial expression, at times suggesting deep unhappiness or utter hopelessness. It is not too much to say that lip reading often seems to bring the light back to the eyes and to put animation and interest into a face that has become only a mask to hide unpleasant thoughts. As the tenseness and the sense of humiliation pass away, relaxed muscles reveal the new feeling of assurance and a new morale is created. The "I can't" complex is replaced by the "I can." Faces become in very truth "amyable and pleausaunt to behold."

Unconsciously many people who cannot readily understand what is being said to them meet the world with a vacant smile. That to be sure is preferable to a vacant frown! What the teacher of lip reading endeavors to do is to make that smile spontaneous and intelligent. Modern text books on lip reading all contain amusing anecdotes and material to provoke smiles, for the true value of humor is recognized. Colleges do not offer courses in humor — essential though it is — nor do schools of lip reading; but humor is constantly put to full use in the work with hard of hearing people.

Wasn't it Aristotle who flunked in giving a definition of humor? Indeed has anyone since given a satisfactory one? Emerson called it "an armament and a safeguard" and asserted that "it defends from the insanities." But after all, analysis will never tell us why a joke is funny. To appreciate humor and to laugh, these are the important matters. Those gifted ones who can make people laugh have a high calling. The humorists of our modern world are very well paid. Gracie Fields, the famous English entertainer, earns something like $750,000 annually. She was honored by King George, receiving the cross of Commander of the Order of the British

Empire. Charlie Chaplin's fortune is said to be a fabulous one.

We deafened people are in general very slow to appreciate jokes. We have an invariable habit of missing the point. In a school of lip reading students are drilled in grasping the meaning of spoken words through the use of funny stories, and such material is used in part for the sake of winning smiles and creating an atmosphere of gaiety. For laughter, of course, has a definite physiological effect. The exercise caused by a hearty laugh is good for us all, especially good for the hard of hearing whose thoughts are prone to dwell upon the serious. Laughter is a contribution to health. It reacts upon the mind and produces a sense of refreshment, of renewal.

From time immemorial the deaf man has himself been the target of jokes and because he is at times so very absurd, the hearing world seems to forget that he has very sensitive feelings. So through the ages he has been made to suffer by the thoughtless. If he can learn to laugh at himself, if he can become the happy possessor of a keen sense of humor, these accomplishments will serve as shield and buckler in time of need. Do you recall that old prayer found in Chester Cathedral where the petitioner prays, "Give me a mind that is not bored, that does not whimper, whine or sigh; don't let me worry overmuch about the fussy thing called I. Give me a sense of humor, Lord, give me the grace to see a joke, and get some happiness from life and pass it on to other folk." The author of that prayer would have made a successful lip reader!

There is a story about a guide in Saint Paul's Church in London. A visitor made some reference to the "Gloomy Dean." The guide promptly corrected him and stated that the Dean deserved no such appellation, that he was merely a "sad hoptimist." There is ample reason why the hard of hearing should feel sad at times but there is also reason why they should learn to hope for the best and to take the optimistic outlook. They know that there is a hole in the doughnut but they likewise know that it need not be emphasized. Their attention can be turned to the good, solid, usable things in their lives and surely it does not require much effort or very profound thought to recognize how truly multitudinous these are. They can deliberately cultivate a sense of humor without which no one's life can be really balanced. Included in the program of all schools of lip reading is the creation of an atmosphere of laughter and optimism. This is the cornerstone on which the morale of the student is raised.

Plainly then the learning of lip reading is a many-faceted jewel. It will lend light to him who wins it for his very own — light not only in the readier comprehension of the spoken word, though this is the practical objective, but also light in the self-confidence that comes with the use of his highest endowments and in the joy that grows with a deeper comprehension of life itself.

Many of us with faulty ears doubt the love and friendship of our relatives and friends. We are unpleasantly aware of the special effort and the unique consideration which we require. We think that we are only a nuisance and a trial to those whose fate it is to associate with us day after day. We wonder if they are more bored or annoyed or wearied by us. We are almost persuaded that no one truly cares about us and we are ready to abandon hope that anyone ever will. To be tolerated, perhaps, is about as much as we can expect. Some such thoughts as these have doubtless passed through the minds of everyone at some period in his deafened life when his faith was burning low.

In a recent number of the Readers Digest a sign that had been seen in a Sussex village in England was printed. The sign read, "Please Drive Slowly. Old Deaf Dog." If the human heart can thus be moved by an old deaf dog, surely no mortal man or woman should doubt its warmth. One of the inalienable privileges of deafness, moreover, is to discover the innate kindness of our fellow beings.

How their patience and forbearance, their thoughtfulness and goodness minister to our slow and awkward ways! If we believe in their affection, if we believe in ourselves, what better course can we follow than to make ourselves worthy? And where are better means to be found than in our magical hearing aids and our cherished attainments in lip reading?

Chapter V

INSTRUCTIONS FOR THE NEW STUDENT

The following exercises are intended primarily to show how much of our speech is readable on the lips and to make the student realize that familiarity with the visible formations of sounds is an essential part of his equipment as an individual with impaired hearing.

Ideally the would-be student of lip reading should pursue a course of lessons with an experienced teacher and should have regular practice, at least during the continuation of his studies. Information concerning private teachers and public school classes in his vicinity and also organizations for the hard of hearing which offer lip reading lessons may be obtained by writing the Volta Bureau, Washington, D. C. If this instruction should be even temporarily impossible, it is believed that these exercises will prove of value as a means of encouraging the student in his efforts to understand the spoken word. They constitute only a suggestion of the work that should later be fully developed and greatly elaborated; but they will give him a basis for work and will convey an idea of the lesson procedure in an accredited school of lip reading.

It is suggested that the student practice the exercises with an assistant even before he reads them over to himself. He will, in all probability, find that he does not understand every word, but if he grasps the meaning, sentence by sentence, he should continue with this form of practice.

If he cannot grasp the thought when the sentences are read to

34   INTRODUCTION TO LIP READING

him, he would do well to practice them with the mirror and then to have the work given by an assistant. In all mirror practice it is important not to exaggerate the movements, but to speak naturally and with careful enunciation. Ten-minute periods of concentrated practice perhaps three times a day will be found of much greater practical value than a single half hour period.

To make this mirror practice intelligent, the student should have an accurate knowledge of how sounds are formed and how they are revealed on the lips; he should therefore consult a standard text on lip reading* in order to obtain this essential foundation for mirror work. He will learn there that vowels are made by shapes of the lips, tongue and throat and that consonants are made by movements of the organs of speech, the result being a constant passing from shape to shape and movement to movement, revealed to the eye chiefly on the lips. In mirror practice the student must always watch for definite shapes and movements, thus forming the essential habit of associating them with the corresponding sound. He should study the following sounds as revealed on the lips in the groups of words given below, remembering that it is not spelling with which he is concerned but sounds and their revelation. In order to see the contrasting revelations he should study the word lists both vertically and horizontally.

The sound for "th" is made by placing the tongue between the teeth, as in "the".

The sounds for "sh" and soft "ch" are revealed by a somewhat

---

*Standard texts on lip reading:
 Nitchie, Edward B., *Lip-Reading — Principles and Practice*, Frederick A. Stokes Co., New York, N. Y., 1912.
 Kinzie, Cora Elsie and Rose, *Lip-Reading for the Deafened Adult*, John C. Winston Co., Chicago, Ill., 1931.
 Bruhn, Martha E., *The Muller-Walle Method of Lip-Reading for the Deaf*, Thomas P. Nichols and Son Co., Lynn, Mass., 1815.
 Bunger, Anna M., *Jena Method of Speech-Reading*, Michigan State Normal College, Ypsilanti, Mich., 1932.

INSTRUCTIONS FOR THE NEW STUDENT   35

square, forward movement of the lips, as in "sheep", "cheap".

The sounds for "m", "b" and "p" are revealed by a closed position of the lips, as in "may", "bay" and "pay". (Although the sound for "m" is nasal, the revelation for the lip reader is the same as for "b" and "p".)

The sound for short "ă" opens the mouth wide and extends the lips, as in "hăm".

The sound for long "ō" tends to bring the lips forward into a rounded shape, as in "hōme".

The sound for long "ē" also extends the lips but makes a very narrow opening between the lips, as in "mē".

The sound for "h" is made with the breath and is not seen on the lips.

The sound for "k" or hard "c" is made in the cavity of the mouth and is not seen on the lips.

Short "ă" Sound	Long "ō" Sound	Long "ē" Sound
Mash	Poach	Peach
Map	Mope	Beam
Sham	Show	Theme
Hath	Both	Heath
Ham	Hope	Heap
Ash	Coach	Each
Cap	Cope	Keep

At the outset the student must clearly understand that he will seldom see every word in a sentence. It is not necessary that he should. He knows the grammar of the English language; he is familiar with the customary rhetorical forms in colloquial speech; and it is assumed that his vocabulary is sufficiently large to enable him to understand the spoken words of an average person. It must be emphasized that the lip reader is reading colloquial speech, not literary dissertations. It is the everyday give and take in the talk of those with whom he is thrown in contact with which he has to deal. His knowledge and also his imagination are brought into play. Let him not hesitate to use both to the fullest possible degree. If, as frequently happens, the use of imagination causes ludicrous mistakes, it is better to continue to use it than not to use it at all.

Lip reading text books for beginners provide an extensive vocabulary of words of one syllable which the student would do well to practice long and thoroughly. He will find, however, that many words of more than one syllable offer him an even better chance to read the lips for the very reason that the lip movement is prolonged. Vocabularies of words of more than one syllable are therefore included in these exercises in order that the student may, from the beginning, form the habit of reading the longer words easily.

Proper nouns constitute one of the major stumbling blocks in lip reading. Those who associate with lip readers know the wisdom of helping with some kind of hint. For example in answer to the lip reader's question, "Who was that on the telephone?", the reply should not be "Mr. Carr," but "Mr. Carr, the upholsterer." Not "Betty", but "Your friend who has the position in the insurance office". If he should ask, "What are you talking about?" you would do him a great favor by answering not just "Gone With the Wind", but "Gone With the Wind, the movie that we saw the other evening".

It is heartening to discover that there are after all a large number of proper nouns that can easily be seen on the lips. Several such vocabularies are given and it will be noted that the great majority of these words are, as it were, on everybody's tongue. The student should master them early.

Whenever vocabularies are being practiced the assistant should give the words one by one, according to the order in the text, asking the student to repeat. He should then change the order until the student has had a thorough drill. Next he should proceed to read the sentences containing the vocabulary words in the text book order.

INSTRUCTIONS FOR THE NEW STUDENT 37

When they have been well mastered, he should read again with a change of order.

We scarcely realize, perhaps, how generally proverbs and quotations are interspersed in our everyday talk, or how often we are quoting the Bible, Shakespeare and Poor Richard. Because of this universal usage, lists of familiar proverbs and quotations are given for practice. They have been chosen because of their wide use but also, in many instances, on account of the ease with which they can be read on the lips. A wise student will familiarize himself with this much-used material. Many times he will find that a single word or phrase will give him the clue that he requires for complete comprehension. Again, he will train himself to be aware of rhythm so that he can quickly recognize poetry with its definite accents and rhymes. This in itself is a clue for the lip reader, an asset that can be put to very good use. Indeed if he is well trained, he will find the rhythm in all spoken language of immeasurable help in making his interpretations.

As those with normal hearing must learn to distinguish between like-sounding words, such as "handsome" and "hansom", or "flower" and "flour", so the lip reader must learn to distinguish between words that have a similar appearance on the lips, such as "summer" and "supper", or "ice" and "eyes." These latter are called *homophenous* words and they constitute a rather large portion of the vocabulary in general use. At first glance this may strike the student as an almost insuperable difficulty but he will soon learn that out of a group of homophenous words his mental processes will tell him which one to choose for the particular context involved. The eye, to be sure, must do its allotted work, but in the end it is the mind that brings the correct reading. All along the way, indeed, it is the psychological side of lip reading that is of paramount importance. While work with homophenous words cannot be called

38 INTRODUCTION TO LIP READING

the easiest form of practice, it is unquestionably one of the most valuable, for it brings into action not only the fundamental eye work but also every function of the mind.

The following suggestions will prove useful to the student's assistant:

1. He should always have the light on his face.
2. He should always speak naturally and clearly, with careful enunciation. Let him beware, however, of exaggeration, of using his tongue too freely, of thrusting his lips forward uncouthly.
3. In the beginning, he should retard his tempo to a slight degree, while still speaking naturally.
4. He should speak in a voice low enough to be inaudible to the student.
5. He should keep his head well up in order that the student may have full opportunity to see the action of the tongue and lips and to observe the facial expression.
6. He should avoid unnatural gesticulation with his hands.
7. He should not repeat single words (except in the vocabulary practice) but should always repeat the entire thought.
8. He should not give an undue amount of repetition, thus causing the student to rely upon this. He may give a word or a sentence as often as three times, perhaps; but if the student fails to understand, he should then show the missed word, in the case of vocabulary practice; and in the case of sentence practice, he should either write the key word or give it in an audible voice, and then repeat the sentence.
9. He should be very careful not to tire the student with too long practice periods. In general forty-five minutes will be found quite adequate at one sitting.
10. A typical practice period might be divided as follows:

INSTRUCTIONS FOR THE NEW STUDENT

1. Rapid review of 25 to 50 in Familiar Colloquial Forms, Section 1.
2. Drill on words with "th", Section 2.
3. A group of ten or more proverbs in advance with a review of those already worked on, Section 3.
4. A group of eight or ten homophenous words, Section 4.
5. Conversation developed from questions in very simple form about some subject in which the student is interested, about his family, about the weather, etc.

40

Chapter VI

LESSONS FOR HOME PRACTICE

Section 1 — Common Colloquial Speech

In all exercises the assistant should show the student the topic. In this section, he should read the sentences in order, giving three chances for each. If the student cannot repeat at the third reading, a key word may be written or audibly spoken. (In Sentence 1 under "The Small Boy Speaks", for instance, the key word is "pie". In Sentence 14 on page 48, the key word is "appointment".) The group should then be reviewed by changing the order of reading and by increasing the tempo up to the maximum that the student can take.

THE SMALL BOY SPEAKS

1. Why can't I have another piece of pie?
2. Why can't I have another ice cream soda?
3. Why can't I have an apple?
4. Why can't I go to the movies?
5. Why can't I go swimming?
6. Why can't I go with you?
7. Why can't I go fishing?
8. Why can't I stay home from school?
9. Why can't I stay up as long as you do?
10. Why can't I take my bath in the morning?
11. Why can't I take my white mouse to school?
12. Why can't I buy some chewing gum?
13. Why can't I have my dog sleep in my room?
14. Why can't I play on the piano?
15. I wish I could go to the ball game.
16. I wish I could stay home from school.
17. I wish I could go fishing.
18. I wish I could wear long trousers.
19. I wish I could drive a car.

LESSONS FOR HOME PRACTICE

20. I wish I had something to eat.
21. I wish I had fifty cents.
22. I wish I was a policeman.
23. I wish I didn't have to go to Sunday School.
24. I did wash my hands with soap.
25. I did brush my teeth before breakfast.
26. I did brush my hair before I came downstairs.
27. I'm not making much noise.
28. I am going to bed.
29. I am telling you the truth.
30. I never told Father a lie.
31. I didn't turn on the water in the bath room.
32. I didn't get my feet wet.
33. I am not teasing Sister.
34. Sister is a cry baby.
35. Sister pinched me.
36. I don't feel very well.
37. I don't want to go to bed.
38. I don't like girls.

THE SMALL GIRL SPEAKS

1. I don't like spinach.
2. I don't like these shoes.
3. I wish I had a new dress.
4. I drank a glass of milk for breakfast.
5. I wish I could have a permanent wave.
6. I don't believe in Santa Claus.
7. I wish I had a baby sister.
8. I want to wear my blue sash.
9. Why can't I stay in bed this morning?
10. Why can't I stay home from Sunday School?
11. Why can't I go to the movies?
12. Why can't I go by myself?
13. Why can't I have another piece of candy?
14. Why is Mother so cross?
15. Why is Brother so mean to me?
16. Why must I keep still?
17. Don't tell Mother what I did.
18. Don't make me wear my overshoes.

42 INTRODUCTION TO LIP READING

19. All the other children are going to the movies.
20. Who made the moon?
21. How old are you?

FAMILIAR COLLOQUIAL FORMS

(1) How are you? (2) How are you feeling this afternoon? (3) Do you feel well? (4) How is your father? (5) How is your mother? (6) Is your mother well? (7) Is your mother sick? (8) How is your brother? (9) How is your sister? (10) How is your wife? (11) How is the baby? (12) How is your husband? (13) How are all the family? (14) We have had a very warm summer. (15) It's very warm this morning. (16) This is a warm day. (17) This is the hottest day we have had this month. (18) This weather is very trying. (19) Do you like warm weather? (20) I always feel well in the summer. (21) It is very warm in the house. (22) It is much cooler out of doors. (23) There is a good breeze out on the porch. (24) The breeze is from the south. (25) It is cool in the shade.

(26) It is very damp this morning (27) There is a heavy fog over the bay. (28) The wind is from the west. (29) The wind is blowing from the northeast. (30) I think we shall have snow. (31) I believe we are going to have a storm. (32) A northeaster is blowing up. (33) We have had so much snow this winter. (34) We have had one snow storm after another. (35) The snow is five inches deep. (36) The boys are making snow balls. (37) The ice on the river is three inches thick. (38) The boys have gone to skate on the river. (39) Do you think it will rain this afternoon? (40) I think it will rain before night. (41) The paper said we would have showers. (42) Those clouds in the west look like rain. (43) I hope it will not rain today. (44) I want to go out for a walk. (45) Do you take a walk every day? (46) Do you ever walk before breakfast? (47) How far can you walk? (48) What time is it? (49) Have you the right time? (50) Have you a watch?

(51) Have you the correct time? (52) My watch is slow. (53) My watch is half an hour slow. (54) My watch does not keep good time. (55) My watch is out of order. (56) What time did you get up this morning? (57) I got up at half past five. (58) Why did you get up so early? (59) I got up to catch the train for Washington. (60) Have you ever been in Washington? (61) Did you go to the White House? (62) Did you see the Washington Monument? (63) Washington is the most beautiful city in the United States. (64) What time does the train leave for Washington? (65) What times does the boat leave the wharf? (66) The ship will sail on Thursday morning at half after eleven. (67) The ferry boat leaves at two o'clock.

LESSONS FOR HOME PRACTICE 43

(68) How long does it take the ferry boat to reach the other side? (69) What time did you have breakfast this morning? (70) We always have breakfast at half past seven. (71) My mother never has breakfast until half past eight. (72) What did you have for breakfast? (73) Did you have fruit? (74) Do you like orange juice for breakfast? (75) I prefer grape fruit.

(76) What kind of cereal will you have? (77) Do you care for oatmeal? (78) Will you have cream and sugar on your oatmeal? (79) Will you have coffee or tea? (80) I am very fond of coffee. (81) I always have two cups of coffee for breakfast. (82) Do you like black coffee? (83) Do you take cream and sugar in your coffee? (84) My grandmother always has tea for breakfast. (85) Is your grandmother an Englishwoman? (86) Can you have lunch with me on Friday? (87) Where shall we go for lunch? (88) What shall we have for lunch? (89) Shall we have hot soup or a fruit cup? (90) Do you care for a lamb chop? (91) Suppose we have lamb chops and peas. (92) Will you have a salad? (93) I think a fruit salad would be very refreshing. (94) What kind of salad dressing do you prefer? (95) French dressing is always nice. (96) Shall we have some strawberry ice cream? (97) I like chocolate better than strawberry. (98) May I have some cheese and crackers? (99) Will you have a small or a large coffee? (100) Please bring me a demi tasse.

(101) Are you going to the post office? (102) Will you mail my letter for me? (103) Shall I bring you some stamps? (104) How many stamps do you want? (105) I want twenty-five two cent stamps and fifty threes. (106) Please get me fifteen post cards and a special delivery stamp. (107) How far is it to the post office? (108) Is the post office very far from here? (109) Can I walk to the post office? (110) Can I go by the street car? (111) The street car runs right by the post office. (112) How long would it take me to walk to the post office? (113) You can easily walk it in half an hour. (114) If you take the street car, you should be there in twelve minutes. (115) How much did you pay for the farm? (116) How large is the farm? (117) How many acres of land have you on the farm? (118) The farm is not very large. (119) We have only seventy-five acres. (120) What do you raise on the farm? (121) Have you any sheep? (122) No, but we have cows and chickens. (123) How far is the farm from the railway station? (124) Have you ever lived on a farm? (125) How would you like to spend the summer on a farm?

(126) Have you ever been on a ranch? (127) I was on a ranch in Wyoming all summer. (128) The ranch was thirty-five miles from the railroad station. (129) The ranch was high up in the mountains. (130) The

weather was perfect all summer. (131) Not too hot and not too cold. (132) I have never seen so many wild flowers in my life. (133) We found forty-five varieties of wild flowers. (135) Do you know many of the wild flowers? (136) What is the name of that large white flower that grows on a bush? (137) Have you any apple trees on the farm? (138) I think the apple blossom is one of the loveliest flowers we have. (139) The rose is my favorite flower. (140) I love the lily of the valley. (141) Have you a flower garden? (142) Do you ever work in your garden before breakfast? (143) How many varieties of flowers have you? (144) I have flowers all summer long. (145) I have flowers from March until November. (146) I suppose you have chrysanthemums in the fall? (147) Where do you live? (148) Where is your home? (149) Do you live in the South? (150) Have you ever lived in the West?

(151) I have always lived in the East. (152) I was born in Massachusetts. (153) My father and my mother were both born in Massachusetts. (154) What is the largest city in Massachusetts? (155) Is Boston the capital of Massachusetts? (156) Do you live in Boston? (157) Is your home in the city or in the suburbs? (158) What is your address? (159) Have you a telephone? (160) What is your telephone number? (161) Shall I call you up this evening? (162) Call me up about seven o'clock. (163) Will you telephone before twelve? (164) Please telephone my wife. (165) I will call up your wife between eleven and twelve. (166) That's fine.

INTERROGATIONS CONTAINING "OR"

1. What shall we have for breakfast?

    (1) Coffee or tea? (2) Oranges or grape fruit? (3) Oatmeal or shredded wheat? (4) Toast or muffins? (5) Boiled eggs or scrambled eggs? (6) Lamb chops or sausage?

2. What shall we have for dinner?

    (1) Soup or tomato juice? (2) Fish or lamb chops? (3) Roast beef or roast lamb? (4) Mashed potatoes or French fried potatoes? (5) Spinach or string beans? (6) Fruit salad or vegetable salad? (7) Apple pie or cherry pie? (8) Ice cream or orange ice? (9) Large or small coffee?

3. What kind of reading do you enjoy most?

    (1) Newspapers or magazines? (2) Prose or poetry? (3) Old-fashioned romance or mystery stories? (4) Biography or history? (5) Short stories or long novels? (6) Essays or books on philosophy?

LESSONS FOR HOME PRACTICE

4. What shall we do this evening?
    (1) Go to the opera or to the theatre? (2) Take a walk or take a drive? (3) Stay at home or go out and make some calls? (4) Play bridge or sit out on the porch? (5) Take a ride on the bus or take a drive in the park? (6) Go to the supper at the church or go for a sail on the bay?

5. Where did that family come from?
    (1) Down South or out West? (2) Alabama or California? (3) The Far West or the Middle West? (4) Washington or Michigan? (5) South Carolina or North Carolina? (6) New Jersey or New York? (7) Massachusetts or New Hampshire? (8) South America or Central America?

6. Where are you going this summer?
    (1) To the seashore or to the mountains? (2) Out West or up North? (3) Fishing in Pennsylvania or motoring in Maine? (4) On a cruise to the West Indies or up the Saint Lawrence River? (5) To Nova Scotia or to the British Isles? (6) To the southwest or to the northwest? (7) Are you going to stay at home or are you going to visit your sister?

7. What kind of weather did you have while you were on the ocean?
    (1) Was it smooth or rough? (2) Was it warm or cold? (3) Did you have sunshine or rain? (4) Did you have stormy weather or smooth sailing? (5) Was the sea as smooth as a mill pond or was it choppy? (6) Did you have heavy fogs or light showers? (7) Was it damp and cold or soft and warm?

8. What kind of hat did she have on?
    (1) Was it large or small? (2) Black or white? (3) Brown or blue? (4) Trimmed with flowers or trimmed with feathers? (5) Did it have a wide brim or a narrow brim? (6) Did it have a high crown or a low crown? (7) Was it made of velvet or of silk? (8) Was it old-fashioned or extremely stylish? (9) Was it new or was it the one she wore all last year?

9. When was she married?
    (1) In June or July? (2) In October or November? (3) In January or February? (4) Before she was twenty or after she was twenty-five? (5) At home or at church? (6) Before she left college or after she was graduated? (7) In the summer or in the fall? (8) When she was in Japan or when she was in China?

10. What is your favorite magazine?

46 INTRODUCTION TO LIP READING

(1) The Saturday Evening Post or the Ladies Home Journal? (2) Life or Punch? (3) Time or Fortune? (4) Harper's Magazine or the Atlantic Monthly? (5) The Geographic or the Readers Digest? (6) The Woman's Home Companion or the Volta Review? (7) Newsweek or the Better Living Magazine?

QUESTIONS WITH VARIOUS ANSWERS

1. Have you any idea how old she is?
   (1) I think she is about forty-five. (2) She is almost fifty. (3) She was forty-two on her last birthday. (4) She is exactly seventeen. (5) She will be sweet sixteen in March. (6) She is past thirty-five. (7) She must be sixty-five if she is a day. (8) She looks much older than she is. (9) She is four years older than her brother. (10) She is older than I am. (11) I haven't any idea how old she is. (12) I haven't the remotest idea.

2. Where was she going when you met her?
   (1) She was going home. (2) She was on her way to the post office. (3) She was going to church. (4) She was on her way to the bank to deposit some money. (5) She was going to the hospital to see a sick friend. (6) She was going to the station to catch a train. (7) She was rushing to a meeting at the Woman's Republican Club. (8) She was going to have lunch with a friend. (9) She was going shopping. (10) She was on her way to the opera. (11) She was going to a matinee. (12) She was starting off on a motor trip.

3. How many children are there in the family?
   (1) They have three children, all boys. (2) There are five children, two boys and three girls. (3) They have six boys and one girl. (4) They have two boys and two adopted daughters. (5) They have a good old-fashioned family of ten, five girls and five boys.

4. How much did you pay for your dress?
   (1) It was very cheap. (2) It was not expensive. (3) It was very inexpensive. (4) I think it was a wonderful bargain. (5) I got it for half price. (6) It was eleven dollars and a half. (7) I paid twelve dollars for it, but it had been marked down. (8) The price was very reasonable. (9) It was very moderate in price. (10) It cost exactly fourteen dollars with the alterations.

5. How is the house situated?
   (1) It is right on the beach. (2) It faces a large open square. (3) It stands on top of a high hill. (4) It is opposite the park. (5) It is

LESSONS FOR HOME PRACTICE

on the east side of the avenue. (6) It stands on the bank of the river. (7) It is not very far from the White House. (8) It is next door to the Presbyterian Church. (9) It is two doors south of the post office. (10) It stands all by itself with its back to the meadows.

6. How did you get to the farm?

(1) We walked all the way. (2) We went by the bus. (3) We drove in the car. (4) We went in grandfather's old-fashioned carriage. (5) We went by train. (6) We made the trip on our bicycles. (7) We traveled twenty-five miles by train and then took the bus. (8) We went by the street car. (9) We went seven miles by street car and walked the rest of the way. (10) We went all the way on horseback.

7. Where did he make his money?

(1) He made his money in the shipping business. (2) He made his money in the automobile business. (3) He made his money in shoes. (4) He made his money building bridges. (5) He made a fortune in oil. (6) He spent twenty-five years in the coffee business in South America. (7) He was a very successful lawyer. (8) He published one book that made a fortune for him. (9) He made a pile of money in the movies. (10) He inherited his fortune from his father.

8. How long have you worn glasses?

(1) Almost all of my life. (2) For over fifty years. (3) I put on glasses when I was five years old. (4) Ever since I was a child. (5) Ever since I was in High School. (6) For something like twenty-five years. (7) For a little over a year. (8) For only four months.

9. Why didn't you invite Mrs. Smith to the bridge party?

(1) Because she can't play bridge. (2) Because she plays such a poor game. (3) Because she wants to talk all the time. (4) Because she pays no attention to the game. (5) Because she is so disagreeable if she doesn't get the prize. (6) Because no one wants to play with her. (7) Because she is always half an hour late. (8) Because I invited her the last time I had a party. (9) Because she always trumps her partner's ace. (10) Because my husband dislikes her so much. (11) Because she almost bores me to death.

10. Why didn't you answer my letter?

(1) I was too busy. (2) I didn't have time. (3) I thought I'd wait until fall. (4) It was simply a matter of procrastination. (5) I guess it's because I am getting lazy. (6) My family letters take all of my spare time. (7) I had rheumatism in my hands so badly that I could not hold a pen. (8) I never got your letter. (9) I did answer your

48 INTRODUCTION TO LIP READING

letter but I sent it to the wrong address. (10) I told my daughter to answer the letter for me, but perhaps she forgot.

11. Why did Jimmie stay home from school?

(1) Because he had the measles. (2) Because he had a sore throat. (3) Because he had a severe cold on his chest. (4) Because his brother had the whooping cough. (5) Because the weather was so bad. (6) Because it was raining so hard. (7) Because the snow was so deep that the roads were impassable. (8) Because he didn't have any overshoes. (9) Because the car was out of order and it was too far to walk. (10) Because he didn't want to go.

"HAVE" IN VARIOUS MEANINGS

1. What did you have for breakfast?
2. They have a large family.
3. How much time have you?
4. Don't have anything to do with that man.
5. Have you read the newspaper this morning?
6. Did you have a pleasant summer?
7. Do you think we shall have rain this afternoon?
8. That woman will always have the last word.
9. You always have your own way.
10. They seem to have so much trouble.
11. Have you ever had the whooping cough?
12. Can you let me have five dollars?
13. I am planning to have some friends for lunch to-morrow.
14. I have an appointment at three o'clock to-morrow afternoon.
15. They have a large apartment on the fifth floor.
16. Will you have a piece of cheese with your pie?
17. You have the advantage of us all.
18. Have you ever read "To Have and To Hold"?
19. They have a way of getting what they want.
20. We have to leave at seven o'clock.
21. Have no fear about your boy.
22. We have a high hill on the north side of the farm.
23. The man must have food or he will starve.
24. I have a feeling that the war won't last very long.
25. The boys both have Spanish but no French.

"OPEN" IN VARIOUS MEANINGS

1. My watch has an open face.

LESSONS FOR HOME PRACTICE

2. Shall I open the door in the dining room?
3. Open your mouth and shut your eyes.
4. May I open the umbrella for you?
5. How shall I open my speech?
6. We always keep open house on New Year's Day.
7. I hope we are going to have an open winter.
8. The house will be open to the public for three weeks.
9. She has a very open mind.
10. That is an open question.
11. The river has been open all through the month of January.
12. That man has a very open countenance.
13. The play opens with a brief prologue.
14. This letter was open when the postman delivered it.
15. How do you feel about the policy of the open door?
16. The professor will give an open lecture in the auditorium.
17. Will you see if you can open this can for me.
18. I did not open my eyes until nine o'clock this morning.
19. The transaction was managed in a very open way.
20. Do you like to sleep out in the open?
21. The man had an open wound for over a month.
22. I think I shall open an account at the fruit shop.
23. They are going to open up a large tract of land along the beach.
24. The invitation will be open until the first of July.
25. It is an open secret that they will be married next year.

GONE WITH THE WIND

(On this exercise, answers should be required.)
1. What is the name of the author of this book?
2. Where is she from?
3. What is this book about?
4. Is it a very long book?
5. How many pages are there?
6. When was it published?
7. Has it been popular, on the best-seller lists?
8. How many copies were sold?
9. Is it an exciting book?
10. Do you think it is well written?
11. Did you enjoy it?
12. Did you find it very absorbing?

INTRODUCTION TO LIP READING

13. How long did it take you to read it?
14. Do you remember the name of the heroine?
15. Is Scarlett the kind of woman that you admire?
16. Was there another woman in the book for whom you had more admiration?
17. What is the name of the hero?
18. Do you believe that the separation of Scarlett and Rhett was final?
19. Do you think this is a true picture of the war period in the South?
20. Has "Gone With The Wind" been made into a moving picture?
21. Who plays the part of Scarlett?
22. Who plays the part of Rhett?
23. Where was the picture shown for the first time?
24. How much do you suppose it cost to produce this picture?
25. By the way, has the author made much money out of this book?
26. How do you think the moving picture compares with the book?

LESSONS FOR HOME PRACTICE 51

SECTION 2 — VOCABULARY AND SENTENCE PRACTICE

Having shown the topic to the student, the assistant should read the vocabulary words in order, asking for repetition. He should read again changing the order. Then giving the vocabulary word first, he should read the sentence in which that word occurs. Finally he should read all of the sentences in changed order.

WORDS HAVING "SH" OR "CH"

SHAMPOO	CHAUFFEUR
CHANGEABLE	FAMISH
CHAMPAGNE	PUBLISH
SHELLFISH	MARSHMALLOW
SHEEPISH	MUSHROOM
SHIPSHAPE	WISHFUL

1. How much do they charge for a shampoo?
2. The weather has been very changeable for the last month.
3. Shall we serve champagne with the dinner?
4. Are you fond of shellfish?
5. The boy has a sheepish expression.
6. The apartment was in shipshape order by half after nine.
7. Our chauffeur has been with us for fifteen years.
8. I thought I would famish before we reached home.
9. He will publish his autobiography this fall.
10. Have you ever made marshmallow fudge?
11. Shall we have mushroom soup for lunch?
12. That child has a very wishful expression.
13. Their charge for a shampoo seems to be rather changeable.
14. We had shellfish for the first course and mushroom soup for the second.
15. He looked very wishful when he saw us open the bottle of champagne.
16. The chauffeur keeps the garage in shipshape order.
17. You will not famish if you eat this mushroom soup.
18. Why has the chauffeur such a sheepish expression?
19. Perhaps the chauffeur drank some of our champagne.
20. If they publish your book, I will give you a five-pound box of marshmallows.

WORDS WITH "TH"

THOUGHTFUL	THERMOMETER
THOUSAND	THEATRICAL
THOROUGHFARE	THANKSGIVING

INTRODUCTION TO LIP READING

BLACKSMITH	MATHEMATICS
FOOTPATH	METHODICAL
CHRYSANTHEMUM	MYTHOLOGY

1. She is the most thoughtful woman I have ever known.
2. I wish I had a thousand dollars.
3. We drove along a wide thoroughfare for about an hour.
4. Have you a thermometer in the office?
5. That was a splendid theatrical performance.
6. Are you going home for Thanksgiving?
7. Who wrote that well-known poem about a blacksmith?
8. We followed the footpath through the woods.
9. That is the largest chrysanthemum I ever saw.
10. I have always been poor in mathematics.
11. The boy is not methodical but he is very bright.
12. Did you study mythology when you were in school?
13. We saw a fine theatrical performance on Thanksgiving afternoon.
14. The old blacksmith has a very thoughtful face.
15. Chrysanthemums were blooming along the thoroughfare.
16. The chrysanthemums will die if the thermometer drops any lower.
17. I like mythology but I do not care much for mathematics.
18. You were very thoughtful to put the thermometer out on the porch.
19. My teacher of mathematics was very methodical.
20. We have a thousand reasons for celebrating Thanksgiving.

GEOGRAPHICAL VOCABULARY

AUSTRALIA	JAPAN
BELGIUM	JAVA
BRITISH EMPIRE	RUSSIA
CHINA	SIAM
EGYPT	HAWAIIAN ISLANDS
GERMANY	PHILIPPINE ISLANDS

1. What is the population of Australia?
2. How long has the King of Belgium been on the throne?
3. Is it true that the sun never sets on the British Empire?
4. China was a civilized country before the birth of Christ.
5. How long were the Children of Israel in the land of Egypt?
6. Have you ever been in Germany?
7. Japan is famous for its cherry trees.
8. They raise very fine coffee in Java.

LESSONS FOR HOME PRACTICE

9. Russia has a very cold climate.
10. What form of government do they have in Siam?
11. How long is the trip from California to the Hawaiian Islands?
12. Are the people of the Philippine Islands much like the Chinese?
13. Australia is a part of the British Empire.
14. How far is Java from Siam?
15. Is Russia very much larger than Germany?
16. How does the population of Belgium compare with that of Egypt?
17. Japan has been making war on China for several years.
18. Which are farther south, the Hawaiian or the Philippine Islands?
19. Have Russia and China been at war in recent years?
20. Belgium and Germany both have seaports on the North Sea.

NAMES OF CITIES

AMSTERDAM	PHILADELPHIA
ATHENS	ROME
BALTIMORE	MINNEAPOLIS
POMPEII (BOMBAY)	SHANGHAI
BUFFALO	SOUTHAMPTON
PARIS	WASHINGTON

1. Amsterdam is a large and important city.
2. Athens has a very beautiful location.
3. Baltimore is on Chesapeake Bay.
4. Have you seen the ruins of Pompeii?
5. Does this ship land at Bombay?
6. What is the population of Buffalo?
7. Paris is a well-known fashion center.
8. Did you see the Liberty Bell when you were in Philadelphia?
9. All roads lead to Rome.
10. The best flour comes from Minneapolis.
11. How would you like to live in Shanghai?
12. We sailed from Southampton on the first of September.
13. Washington is the most beautiful city in America.
14. How far is it from Paris to Amsterdam?
15. Is it possible to fly from Amsterdam to Athens?
16. We went from Paris to Rome by rail.
17. We motored from Rome to Pompeii in something like four hours.
18. The ship sailed from Southampton to Shanghai.
19. I have been in Rome but I have never been in Athens.

INTRODUCTION TO LIP READING

20. It is three hours from Philadelphia to Washington by rail.
21. I stopped off at Buffalo on my way to Minneapolis.
22. Is there a bus that runs from Washington to Baltimore?
23. Is Minneapolis as large as Philadelphia?
24. Rome is the capital of Italy and Paris is the capital of France.
25. Would you rather live in Washington or Philadelphia?

MONTHS AND SEASONS

JANUARY	JULY	WINTER
FEBRUARY	AUGUST	SPRING
MARCH	SEPTEMBER	SUMMER
APRIL	OCTOBER	FALL
MAY	NOVEMBER	AUTUMN
JUNE	DECEMBER	

1. April showers bring May flowers.
2. Thirty days hath September.
3. Christmas comes on the twenty-fifth of December.
4. The month of August is usually very warm.
5. October is a beautiful month in the mountains.
6. George Washington was born on the twenty-second of February.
7. The apple trees will be in bloom by the latter part of May.
8. The schools all close during the month of June.
9. Armistice Day falls on the eleventh of November.
10. How are you going to celebrate the Fourth of July?
11. March is a very windy month in the North.
12. Are there thirty-one days in January?
13. I should love to go South for the three winter months.
14. "In the spring a young man's fancy lightly turns to thoughts of love".
15. "If winter comes can spring be far behind?"
16. The Last Rose of Summer is a beautiful old song.
17. Football is a popular autumn sport.
18. The fall is a busy time for boys and girls who go away to school
19. Washington has not a very good climate in the summer.
20. Thousands of people spend the summer months at the shore.

DAYS OF THE WEEK and TIME PHRASES

SUNDAY	THURSDAY	AFTERNOON	NOON
MONDAY	FRIDAY	EVENING	MIDNIGHT
TUESDAY	SATURDAY	NIGHT	WEEK
WEDNESDAY	MORNING	DAWN	WEEK-END

LESSONS FOR HOME PRACTICE

1. Can you meet me after church on Sunday morning?
2. Can you meet me on Monday morning at eleven?
3. Can you meet me at six-thirty on Tuesday?
4. Can you meet me Wednesday morning at half after seven?
5. I cannot meet you before ten on Thursday morning.
6. I cannot meet you until Friday.
7. I will meet you at four o'clock on Saturday afternoon.
8. I shall be delighted to have lunch with you on Tuesday of next week.
9. I shall be delighted to have tea with you at four this afternoon.
10. I should love to come for lunch next Monday at one.
11. Will you be at home on Friday afternoon about three o'clock?
12. Will you be at home on Tuesday morning of next week?
13. May I come to see you on Thursday evening?
14. May I come to see you right after lunch on Friday?
15. I shall be at home all day Monday.
16. I am always at home on Wednesday afternoons.
17. I hope to be at home on Sunday from four until seven.
18. I expect to be at home on Wednesday and Friday afternoons of this week.
19. I shall be at home every afternoon of next week except Tuesday.
20. I can see you either Friday morning or Thursday afternoon.
21. We shall sail for the West Indies at noon on Thursday.
22. We expect to be away about a fortnight.
23. I woke up at dawn this morning.
24. I did not go to sleep until after midnight.
25. They are planning to spend the week-end at Atlantic City.

56 INTRODUCTION TO LIP READING

SECTION 3 — QUOTATIONS AND PROVERBS

The quotations and proverbs should be read in textual order. When the student can repeat accurately, the assistant may add interest to the lesson by giving another familiar saying or by making some pertinent comment or by using the saying as a basis for brief conversation with frequent questions. In the exercise on Shakespeake he should ask the student to answer the questions if possible, but not to repeat them.

1. Baa, baa, black sheep, have you any wool?
2. Mary had a little lamb
   Its fleece was white as snow.
3. Pussy cat, pussy cat, where have you been?
4. Jack and Jill went up the hill
   To fetch a pail of water.
5. The north wind doth blow and we shall have snow.
6. How doth the little busy bee improve each shining hour?
7. Old King Cole was a merry old soul.
8. All the king's horses and all the King's men
   Couldn't put Humpty Dumpty to-gether again.
9. Dickory, dickory dock
   The mouse ran up the clock.
10. "I doubt it", said the carpenter and shed a bitter tear.
11. Old Mother Hubbard went to the cupboard
    To get her poor dog a bone.
12. All is fair in love and war.
13. Birds of a feather flock together.
14. Fine feathers make fine birds.
15. Half a loaf is better than no bread.
16. Never put off until to-morrow that which you can do to-day.
17. People who live in glass houses shouldn't throw stones.
18. If at first you don't succeed, try, try again.
19. Pride goeth before a fall.
20. Procrastination is the thief of time.
21. Time and tide wait for no man.
22. When the cat is away the mice will play.
23. Where there's a will, there's a way.
24. Where there's life, there's hope.
25. I stood on the bridge at midnight.
26. Under a spreading chestnut-tree
    The village smithy stands.

LESSONS FOR HOME PRACTICE

27. Listen, my children, and you shall hear
Of the midnight ride of Paul Revere.
28. Tell me not in mournful numbers
Life is but an empty dream.
29. O say, can you see by the dawn's early light?
30. My bonnie lies over the ocean.
31. 'Tis better to have loved and lost
Than never to have loved at all.
32. Full many a flower is born to blush unseen.
33. Home is the sailor, home from the sea.
34. O, my love's like a red, red rose.
35. Gather ye rose buds while ye may.
36. A primrose by a river's brim
A yellow primrose was to him
And nothing more.
37. The Lord is my shepherd; I shall not want.
38. I will lift up my eyes unto the hills from whence cometh my help.
39. Bless the Lord, O my soul and all that is within me.
40. Let the words of my mouth and the meditation of my heart be acceptable in thy sight, O Lord my strength and my redeemer.
41. O worship the Lord in the beauty of holiness.
42. It is a good thing to give thanks unto the Lord.
43. The fear of the Lord is the beginning of wisdom.
44. They that sow in tears shall reap in joy.
45. A wise son maketh a glad father.
46. A soft answer turneth away wrath.
47. Where there is no vision the people perish.

HOW MUCH DO YOU KNOW ABOUT SHAKESPEARE?

1. Where was Shakespeare born?
2. In what year was he born?
3. In what month was he born?
4. What was his father's name?
5. What was his father's occupation?
6. Whom did Shakespeare marry?
7. How old was he when he was married?
8. Was his wife older or younger than he was?
9. How many children did they have?
10. Did all of the children live to grow up?

58 INTRODUCTION TO LIP READING

11. What was Shakespeare's age when he left home and went up to London?
12. How did he earn his living at first?
13. Can you tell me how many plays Shakespeare wrote?
14. Have you ever read any of his love poems?
15. How old was Shakespeare when he died?
16. Where was he buried?
17. Would you say that Shakespeare had a very large vocabulary?
18. Are Shakespeare's plays absolutely original?
19. Have you ever seen a play of Shakespeare's?
20. Have you ever seen Hamlet?
21. Who played the part of Hamlet?
22. Which do you think is the greater play, Hamlet or Macbeth?
23. How many of Shakespeare's plays have you read?
24. Have you a statue of Shakespeare in the city where you live?
25. There is a statute of Shakespeare in Central Park, New York City.

QUOTATIONS FROM SHAKESPEARE

1. To be, or not to be: that is the question.
2. To die, to sleep; to sleep; perchance to dream: ay, there's the rub.
3. All that glitters is not gold.
4. It is a wise father that knows his own son.
5. If you have tears, prepare to shed them now.
6. Brevity is the soul of wit.
7. Lord, what fools these mortals be!
8. How far that little candle throws his beams.
9. One touch of nature makes the whole world kin.
10. Some are born great, some achieve greatness, and some have greatness thrust upon 'em.
11. Good night, good night! parting is such sweet sorrow.
12. Friends, Romans, countrymen, lend me your ears.
13. The evil that men do lives after them
The good is oft interr'd with their bones.
14. This above all, to thine own self be true.
15. Something is rotten in the state of Denmark.
16. Sweet are the uses of adversity.
17. Like patience on a monument, smiling at grief.
18. When shall we three meet again?
19. The quality of mercy is not strained.
20. Yon Cassius hath a lean and hungry look.
21. What's in a name? That which we call a rose
By any other name would smell as sweet.

LESSONS FOR HOME PRACTICE

Section 4 — Homophenous Words

In giving the drill on homophenous words, the assistant should permit the student to read the group of words on which he is to be drilled and should then repeat them so that their similarity on the lips may be carefully observed. He should then read the sentences in the given order, finally changing the order for rapid review. If he has drilled, for example, on seven groups of homophenes, he can finish the work with sentences chosen here and there among the various groups. As the student becomes more proficient in this work, the assistant may find that he can give the drill by writing only one word out of the group of homophenous words thus letting the thought suggest the other homophenes. He will find that words will be more impressed on the student's mind if he asks him to write the words as he understands them.

BLUE, BLEW
1. The sky is very blue this afternoon.
2. The baby has large, blue eyes.
1. The wind almost blew me off my feet.
2. The wind blew from the south.

BUSH, PUSH
1. That is a beautiful rose bush.
2. I found five roses on the bush.
1. Please don't push me like that.
2. The man tried to push me off the platform.

BROWN, PROUD
1. My mother has brown eyes.
2. Who lives in that old, brown house?
1. She is a very proud woman.
2. He is very proud of his family.

CHIP, SHIP
1. That woman has a chip on her shoulder.
2. He is a chip off the old block.
1. What time will the ship arrive at the wharf?
2. The ship will sail on Thursday morning.

CHAIR, SHARE
1. This is the most expensive chair we have.
2. That chair belonged to my grandmother.
1. The boy had more than his share.
2. Will you share your umbrella with me?

60 INTRODUCTION TO LIP READING

CHARM, SHARP
1. She has more charm than anyone I know.
2. This charm is made of solid gold.
1. The boy has very sharp eyes.
2. A sharp wind is blowing from the west.

CHATTER, SHATTER
1. The children chatter all day long.
2. I wonder what they chatter about.
1. That boy will shatter his mother's hopes.
2. Have you shatter-proof glass in your car?

FAIR, FARE
1. That man is always fair.
2. What did you think of the World's Fair?
1. What is the fare to Washington?
2. I will pay your fare on the bus.

FEEL, VEAL
1. How do you feel this morning?
2. Do you feel like going for a swim?
1. Will you have a veal chop?
2. How much is veal a pound?

FIVE, FIFE
1. There are five boys in the family.
2. I got up at half past five this morning.
1. Can you play on the fife?
2. This fife belonged to my grandfather.

FLOWER, FLOUR
1. The rose is my favorite flower.
2. Have you been to the flower show?
1. How much is flour a pound?
2. Do you use white flour or whole wheat flour?

HOME, HOPE
1. There is no place like home.
2. What time will you be at home this evening?
1. While there's life, there's hope.
2. They hope to be married next month.

HANDSOME, HANSOM
1. She is a very handsome woman.
2. Who is that handsome man you were talking to?
1. Did you ever ride in a hansom cab?
2. Hansom cabs are not used very much any more.

LESSONS FOR HOME PRACTICE

HILL, ILL
1. There is a high hill back of the farm.
2. Shall we walk to the top of the hill?
1. The baby is very ill this morning.
2. I never felt so ill in my life.

ICE, EYES
1. Will you have some ice tea?
2. There is no ice in the refrigerator.
1. Have you ever had any troubles with your eyes?
2. She has the most beautiful eyes I ever saw.

LAD, LAND
1. The lad with the blue eyes is my brother.
2. When he was a lad of fifteen, he was very handsome.
1. This land is very valuable.
2. What time will the boat land?

LACE, LAYS
1. That is a beautiful piece of lace.
2. How much is that lace by the yard?
1. She always lays her wraps on the sofa.
2. Have you ever read "The Lays of Ancient Rome?"

MANY, PENNY
1. How many people are in this room?
2. There's many a slip twixt the cup and and the lip.
1. A penny for your thoughts.
2. That woman is penny wise.

MEMBER, PEPPER
1. Are you a member of the church?
2. I am a member of the Republican Club.
1. Please pass me the pepper.
2. It was the pepper that made me sneeze.

MENTION, PENSION
1. Please do not mention this to anyone.
2. There is no reason to mention my name.
1. He has a very large pension.
2. She will receive a pension after she is sixty-five.

OPEN, OMEN
1. Open your mouth and shut your eyes.
2. Please open the window in the bath room.
1. Do you think that is a bad omen?
2. Is it a bad omen to open an umbrella in the house?

INTRODUCTION TO LIP READING

PROFIT, PROPHET
1. Our profit was not very large.
2. They made a profit of five hundred dollars.
1. Are you a good weather prophet?
2. Have you read the book of the prophet Jeremiah?

POISE, BOYS
1. She has more poise than her mother.
2. She has poise but she is very homely.
1. How many boys are there in the Freshman class?
2. The boys will be home on the first of June.

PROVE, PROOF
1. You can't prove that by me.
2. Can you prove this problem?
1. The first proof was not very satisfactory.
2. The proof of the pudding is in the eating.

RICE, RISE
1. Shall we have boiled rice for supper?
2. The Chinese eat a great deal of rice.
1. What time did the sun rise this morning?
2. The farmer and his wife rise very early in summer.

RHYME, RIPE
1. Can you give me a word that will rhyme with giraffe?
2. I see neither rhyme nor reason in that proposition.
1. These apples are not very ripe.
2. The man reached a ripe old age.

RUB, RUM
1. Ay, there's the rub.
2. Why do you rub your eyes so much?
1. Where does the best rum come from?
2. Do you like the flavor of rum?

SHAME, SHAPE
1. It is a shame to waste your time.
2. It is a shame to keep you waiting so long.
1. The woman's hat has a very queer shape.
2. The shape of that vase is absolutely perfect.

SUMMER, SUPPER
1. We spent the summer at the seashore.
2. The summer has been warm and dry.
1. What shall we have for supper?
2. The boy went to bed without any supper.

LESSONS FOR HOME PRACTICE

BILL, MILL, PILL
1. Shall I send you a bill?
2. I will pay the bill on the first of the month.
1. We can walk to the mill in half an hour.
2. Have you ever read the "Mill on the Floss"?
1. The pill rolled under the sofa.
2. The pill is too large for the child to swallow.

BUFF, MUFF, PUFF
1. Why don't you wear your buff dress?
2. Do you like the combination of buff and blue?
1. My muff is very shabby.
2. This was a very expensive muff.
1. It makes me puff to walk up hill.
2. Have you a powder puff in your bag?

EAR, HEAR, HERE
1. She has a wonderful ear for music.
2. The man is very deaf in his left ear.
1. What do you hear from home?
2. Can you hear the telephone?
1. What time can you be here in the morning?
2. The boat will be here before six o'clock.

HARM, HARP, ARM
1. There is no harm in drinking a glass of wine.
2. She did not mean to do you any harm.
1. She plays the harp unusually well for a woman.
2. Why do you harp on that subject?
1. My arm is longer than yours.
2. I broke my arm last summer.

LAMB, LAMP, LAP
1. Mary had a little lamb.
2. Shall we have lamb chops for lunch?
1. They have an old-fashioned oil lamp at the farm.
2. Will you light the lamp in the hall?
1. The boy sat on his father's lap.
2. They live in the lap of luxury.

RABBIT, RAPID, RABID
1. The boys have a little white rabbit.
2. What does the rabbit eat?
1. The boys made rapid progress in school.
2. The man was walking at a rapid pace.

INTRODUCTION TO LIP READING

1. She is rabid on the subject of communism.
2. I don't believe that I am rabid about anything.

ROPE, ROBE, ROAM

1. Did you ever skip rope when you were a child?
2. How much would I have to pay for twelve feet of rope?
1. Grandmother has a warm lounging robe.
2. Have you a laprobe in the automobile?
1. I'd like to roam in the woods this afternoon.
2. This is a very wet day to roam in the woods.

WHERE, WEAR, WARE

1. Where was George Washington born?
2. I don't know where that boy can be.
1. What are you going to wear on board ship?
2. That material will wear very well.
1. That is a beautiful Japanese ware.
2. Is this ware very expensive?

WISH, WITCH, WHICH

1. What do you wish for most of all?
2. I hope your wish will come true.
1. She was dressed like an old witch.
2. I wish I could find a story about an old witch.
1. Which boy won the prize at school?
2. I don't know which hat would be most becoming.

BEES, PEAS, PEACE, PIECE

1. Have you many bees at the farm?
2. The bees are swarming this afternoon.
1. Will you shell the peas for supper?
2. Those are the largest sweet peas I ever saw.
1. There is no peace in that family.
2. All the world longs for peace.
1. Will you have a piece of cheese with your pie?
2. We bought a small piece of property at the beach.

BUY, BY, MY, PIE

1. Do you think they will buy the farm?
2. I must buy myself a pair of shoes.
1. The baby can walk all by himself.
2. I will be home by seven o'clock.
1. My wife has gone South for the winter.
2. How would you like to be in my place?
1. Father is very fond of apple pie.

LESSONS FOR HOME PRACTICE

    2. Will you have pie or ice cream?

BORE, MORE, PORE, POUR

    1. Will you bore a hole in this wood for me?
    2. He is the worst bore I ever met.
    1. The more we have, the more we want.
    2. She is much more selfish than her sister.
    1. A pore is a very small opening, as in the skin.
    2. A leaf also has a pore.
    1. Will you pour the coffee for me?
    2. I thought it would pour before we reached home.

CHOOSE, CHEWS, SHOES, JUICE

    1. If you could choose a trip, where would you go?
    2. I think I would choose a trip to South America.
    1. That boy chews gum all the time.
    2. The baby chews his food very well.
    1. Those shoes are too tight for you.
    2. Have you a pair of heavy walking shoes?
    1. These oranges don't seem to have very much juice.
    2. Do you ever take hot water and lemon juice before breakfast?

MAN, MAT, MAD, MANNED

    1. He was an honest man and very warm-hearted.
    2. Ask that man to show you the way.
    1. There was a small mat under the lamp on the table.
    2. Did you wipe your shoes on the door mat?
    1. Surely that was a mad thing to do.
    2. Do you think that Hamlet was really mad?
    1. The ship was not very well manned.
    2. The ship must be fully manned before it can leave port.

PLAID, PLAN, PLANNED, PLANT

    1. That plaid dress is very becoming to you.
    2. I have an old plaid shawl that was my grandmother's.
    1. How do you feel about this plan?
    2. I think the plan is excellent.
    1. Have you planned to go away this summer?
    2. We have planned to spend the summer on a ranch.
    1. Will you help me plant these flower seeds?
    2. This plant came from Japan.

BADGE, BATCH, MATCH, PATCH, MASH

    1. Why are you wearing that red badge?
    2. This is the badge of a society that I belong to.

INTRODUCTION TO LIP READING

1. I found this batch of mail on the doorstep.
2. Father always has a heavy batch of mail.
1. She made a very poor match.
2. That boy is more than a match for me.
1. The boy has a patch on the seat of his trousers.
2. The man had a patch over his left eye.
1. How did you mash your finger?
2. Shall I mash the potatoes for lunch?

ROAN, ROAD, RODE, ROTE, ROWED, WROTE

1. How old is that roan horse?
2. The roan horse is very valuable.
1. There is a good road all the way to the farm.
2. We found these flowers beside the road.
1. I rode a bicycle when I was about fifteen.
2. We rode horseback all summer.
1. I know that poem by rote.
2. She does the housework by rote.
1. The boy rowed the boat for two miles.
2. He rowed very well for such a small boy.
1. Who wrote the Psalms?
2. He wrote that book before he was twenty years old.

PALM, BALM, POMP, BOB, MOP, POP, MOB

1. Have you ever sat under a palm tree?
2. The palm of my hand is very rough.
1. Those words are balm to my soul.
2. Have you any balm among your flowers?
1. Why was there so much pomp on that occasion?
2. I see no reason for all this pomp.
1. When did you bob your hair?
2. We watched the little boat bob up and down on the water.
1. Please mop up the floor before breakfast.
2. You will find a mop behind the kitchen door.
1. Shall we pop some corn for the children?
2. I thought my eyes would pop out of my head.
1. There was an angry mob in front of the bank this morning.
2. There is always a mob in the subway.